More
than a Memory

Carol J. Grace

authorHOUSE®

AuthorHouse™
1663 Liberty Drive
Bloomington, IN 47403
www.authorhouse.com
Phone: 1-800-839-8640

© 2010 Carol J. Grace. All rights reserved.

No part of this book may be reproduced, stored in a retrieval system, or
transmitted by any means without the written permission of the author.

First published by AuthorHouse 12/07/2010

ISBN: 978-1-4520-5330-1 (sc)
ISBN: 978-1-4520-5331-8 (e)

Library of Congress Control Number: 2010913651

Printed in the United States of America

This book is printed on acid-free paper.

Because of the dynamic nature of the Internet, any Web addresses or links contained in
this book may have changed since publication and may no longer be valid. The views
expressed in this work are solely those of the author and do not necessarily reflect the
views of the publisher, and the publisher hereby disclaims any responsibility for them.

Photo of Carol J. Grace done by Photography by Melisa, Little Rock, Arkansas.

Comments from readers

Your poetry touches something deep inside each and every woman of our generation and beyond. As I read your work, it is so rewarding to recognize things familiar, but even more, to realize things overlooked and rarely mentioned. You bring to light the inner recesses of a woman's soul.

Jo Lea Levy, DDS, Alexandria, LA

The Chinese have a saying, "a poem in every painting, a painting in every poem." With the stroke of her pen, Carol Grace skillfully paints many pictures with her words. *More than a Memory* by Carol Grace is more than just memories. It is about remembering the past, connecting with the present, and looking to the future with faith. It is like standing on the line of time looking back to see where you've been, looking around to see where you are, and looking forward to see where life's journey will take you.

More than a Memory is a wonderful collection of Carol's reflections and perspectives that begin in the memories of the mind and takes you to the very heart and soul of the human journey. "'Tis grace has bro't me safe thus far, and grace will lead me home."

Linda James Southern (James Family Singers)

Acknowledgement

Some of the poems in this book have appeared in both online publications and in print. They are:

The Maumelle Monitor
    Act One
    River of Words
Dawn-Star, online magazine
    Down but not out
Epiphany, online magazine
    I Walk the Road Straight
Adhara, online magazine
    Defining Moments
    A Young Girl Remembered (re-titled A Young Woman Remembered)
Menagerie, online magazine
    Cicada Time in Richmond
    Honking Geese
Snapdragon, online magazine
    Sunset
    Under the Banyan Tree

I would like to thank my nephew, Drew Thompson, for proof-reading my manuscript, along with Jo Lea Levy, Linda James Southern, Harding Stedler, Ralph Hyman, and John Marshall for their kind comments.

Contents

Part 2: Faith   40

Foreword

When I began reading Carol Grace's new collection of poems, I was intent on writing a book myself. So, reading her book provided me with some lessons I could apply in writing my own. What I did in reading her manuscript was to take writing lessons, borrowing from all five divisions of her collection.

I knew going into this venture that it takes good words to make good poems. Many of Carol's poems provided me with examples of how to employ graphic action verbs, especially in the poems "Always keep the screen door locked" and "Best Laid Plans."

Aptly chosen words steered me in the direction of wanting to use vivid sensory images. In her poem "Has it been twenty-five years," words such as *glints*, *pronounced*, and *stench* define the poem. And in a later poem, "Defining Moments," words like *radiance*, *threshold*, and *shrillness* do likewise.

I came to appreciate how dialogue, when used to spell the narration, can enrich and enliven a poem. Dialogue clearly does that in "The Fine Art of Communication" where the spoken word shows rather than tells. And what better way to end the poem "...and your sons and your daughters will prophesy" than with spoken word?

Although I am not an avid fan of rhyme, several of the poems use rhyme in novel ways here and have a way of pulling the reader more deeply into the poem. Such was the case in Carol's poem "The Last Word" where the rhymes appear in both consecutive and alternating patterns in the same poem, keeping the reader alert. The couplet stanzas in "What a difference a day makes" keeps the reader on task as he makes his way--predictably--from beginning to end.

Comparisons always make for good poetic lines, and we have ample evidence of their effectiveness in a number of locations here.

In "Changing the world is easier said than done," the poet effectively opens her poem with the simile

> *we wore our hope like a badge*
> *pinned tightly to our vest.*

Then she begins her second strophe with yet another comparison:

> *We set our faces like flint and our*
> *shoulders firmly against the stone...*

Just as effectively in "The Word Dance," she begins her poem with two similes in the opening strophe:

> *Fever spikes like pitchforks*
> *and words flit before my eyes*
> *like grazing butterflies.*

Poems that define can be equally effective. In her poem "Best Friends," Carol defines what a best friend is over the course of the entire poem. And in "Riding the Rails," the entire poem describes **poetry**.

More than a Memory is both a pleasure to read and is instructional and informative for readers who might someday like to pen their own collection of poems.

Harding Stedler, Poet, Retired Professor
Maumelle, AR

"I have been studying the difference
between solitude and loneliness,
telling the story of my life
to the clean white towels taken warm from the dryer."

Richard Jones[1]

A poet is, before anything else, a person who is passionately in love
with language.
W. H. Auden[2]

Ephesians 1:16 (New International Version)
[16]I have not stopped giving thanks for you, remembering you in my prayers.

Introduction

In one of her less memorable works, Jane Austen ironically says this about memories:

> *If any one faculty of our nature may be called more wonderful than the rest, I do think it is memory. There seems something more speakingly incomprehensible in the powers, the failures, the inequalities of memory, than in any other of our intelligences. The memory is sometimes so retentive, so serviceable, so obedient, at others, so bewildered and so weak, and at others again, so tyrannic, so beyond control! We are, to be sure, a miracle every way, but our powers of recollecting and of forgetting do seem peculiarly past finding out.*

Jane Austen, Mansfield Park[3]

In this, my second book of poetry, most of the poems are less introspective than in *Reflections of a Life Well Spent* and deal more with every day observations. *More than a Memory* offers the simple joy of letting words spill from my thoughts and onto paper.

I have had a love affair with words all of my life, and poetry to me is more than a release, more than therapy. Poetry happens when thought becomes image, image becomes word, and words join together to form meaning that is often unique to each reader.

It is my hope that *More than a Memory* will trigger your own fond memories, and moreover, that you would be encouraged, if not challenged, to continue to make new memories, not letting the days get away from you. As Thoreau said, "How vain it is to sit down to write when you have not stood up to live." [4]

Part One: Tapestry

Puzzling, isn't it?

For some people life is like
a tapestry, events woven
in brightly colored threads
all coming together
in the end.

For me, life is more like
a jigsaw puzzle, strewn
haphazardly on the table
and I search frantically
for the corners, hoping
to find an anchor that
will prevent me from
drifting, seeking the
straight lines to provide
definition to a life
that has tried, and
just keeps trying
to finish the puzzle.

Moments With My Father

Sitting in his room late at night, just
the green glow of the radio and the tip

of his cigarette burning orange, listening
to "Mack the Knife," a tenuous sense

of security washing over me, knowing
that my growing up and his growing old

would soon grow us apart.

Not All Chickens Come Home to Roost

Cousin Harold used to wrestle alligators
down there in Cajun land, while
I grapple with my own type of gator.

Depression does not rest long
in my house, for I will not abide
his company, not allow for his

intrusive presence to manifest
himself in my everyday schemes.
But sometimes when I am not

alert, he sneaks in the back door
as he has done to so many of my
family before, and once he

has arrived, he tends to nest.
So I muster the courage
to look him in the eye

and call him what he is,
the destroyer of lives, the
procrastinator of plans,

and I wrestle him to the ground
until he begs for release,
eager to escape my unyielding

grasp, and I stand astride him,
just another alligator struck down
by me and cousin Harold.

I'll Fly Away

Little twin girls sitting
in their little twin rockers,
wearing little twin nightgowns,
eyes still yielding to sleep.

Daddy, leaning over,
crouching down, crying,
saying, "Aunt Mamie
can't come see you today,
she had to fly away."

"No, she didn't, Daddy,"
my voice strong and
sure. "She promised
she would come."

Mama, in the corner crying,
glancing out through
grief-filled handkerchief.

Aunt Mamie would not
be here today, not today
nor any more days. She flew
away, oh, glory, she
flew away.

Always keep the screen door locked

The wind swooshed in and the
dandelions did cartwheels
across the yard, while laundry
snapped to attention
on the line dancing just
outside the back door.

The rain drops were the size
of quarters as they slapped
the sheets, then the towels, and
she ran to bring them
in, to salvage at least
part of her day's work.

We sat in our little
chairs, singing and rocking
while she whacked on the screen door,
arms filled with dry sheets turning
wet, she begged, but we did
not unlock the door.

And we sang:
Bringing in the sheets,
bringing in the sheets,
we shall come rejoicing
bringing in the sheets.

Salvation

Circus tent, a dirty white,
pitched out there on
Asher Avenue, traveling preacher

come to save our souls, screaming
about fire and brimstone and, "Don't you
want to go to Heaven, little girl?"

Surrounded
by men, women, faces contorted,
shouting

to God as though He were deaf,
she rushed
down to the makeshift altar, down

to where the sinners lined up to receive
a blessing, not wanting to cry,
but afraid not to, afraid

they would think
she really was a sinner,
when she was just a little girl.

Death by Typewriter

It was a 1964 Chevrolet Corvair,
my first car, white with red
vinyl interior. I loved that little
automobile. After all, it gave
me my first flavor of freedom.

Like the Volkswagen, the engine
rode in the back, displacing the trunk
and confounding mechanics everywhere.
Unlike the Volkswagen, accidents piled high
while safety records plummeted.

So, in 1965 with just a few strokes
from the typewriter keys, Ralph
Nader, that self-professed savior
of consumer safety, sentenced my
little car to death.

It was not a pretty sight to see
my faithful car limp off to be
hanged by the carburetor until
dead. I have had a lot of cars,
but none like that first little Corvair.

Best Friends

He has been my best friend
for most of my life—not all
of my life, that's not the way
it works, not when your brother
is seven years younger
and decidedly a pest.

But pest evolved into best as we
became adults, both headstrong
and with a passion for music
and acting (he in the spotlight,
me in the dark, part of the collective
experience we call theater).

We do not always agree,
but we do not have to—that
is not what being best friends
is all about. Best friends
is trusting he will always
have my best interest
at heart, knowing he will
always be there when
I call.

Who Knew?

Groundhog Day means different things
to different people

For me, it was the day she became lost to me,
if not forever, at least for a long time to come.
She was the same age then that I am now--
how odd.

Thirty-five years and her features are now mine,
her consciousness still living deep within my soul,
I carry her with me wherever I go--
how comforting.

I see her face clearly, her blue eyes bright
and peering into my thoughts, but her voice
gone for now, can't recall the sound--
how sad.

Thirty-five years and counting, who knew
this much time would elapse, who knew I could
miss her this much?

Who knew?

My Hiding Place

You are my hiding place,
the one I run to, seek solace in when
life takes a wrong turn and

I end up on a dead end street,
you are there to draw me a map
on a napkin, to point me

in the right direction, to shelter
me from the winds of change
and the storms of indecision.

You are my hiding place.

Smile though you're feeling blue

for Larry, Happy Father's Day 2008

Some people are drawn in by the eyes,
supposedly the porthole to the soul,
but for me it was your smile,
accepting, loving, making me
at last feel whole.

Some people would walk a mile for a Camel,
but I would walk that far and more
to bask in your smile,
the chance to linger
at your door

and know that I was the creator of the radiance
that set your face aglow,
that when you saw me
you could not help but
beam, your face a tableau

of all you say, and think, and do, and everything
it seems at last transpires
to soothe me to some degree,
to replenish and nourish, it is
all my solitary soul requires.

Speaking of the Past

I open the drawer of memories,
some in color, some black and white,
fragments of time forever held
captive, prisoners chained
in my bedroom awaiting
a visit from their warden.

I always intend to sort through
these relics of funny hairdos
and strange looking shoes,
put them in order, and bind
them together to preserve
and keep them.

It never happens.

Instead, I become engrossed
in my yesteryears, absorbed
in the array of now and forever
while my own personal time machine
transports me to 1980, 1957, 1940
and beyond, these tightly held

mementos loosely stacked together,
some faded with creases
and dog-eared corners,
but each bearing images
of people, events, places all kept
safely in the drawer where I store
my youth, each one united
at last, whispering of the past
and all they have seen and done,
secure in the confines of Kodak paper.

Used to Be

My used to be list is getting too long, with
a few things I just don't think belong.
I used to be able with little regard
to hit a driver almost 200 yards, and
dance until midnight and stay up playing
cards.

I drank coffee until late and then
slept the night through, the caffeine never
causing even one jitter or two.
From my used to be list one thing is quite clear,
the things I can do are dwindling I fear,
until one day my "used to be's" will be
the only ones that matter,
for my "I can do" list
will include only chatter.

The Birthday Wish

Thirty candles on a birthday cake
do not begin to tell the story
of your life or mine.

In one morning, my life changed
forever. Once you are called
Mom nothing is ever the same.

I may have given you life,
but you gave me the joy of
living.

I may have met your needs,
but you fulfilled the desires
of my heart.

As a child, you had a love of life
that was unsurpassed and a
laugh that was infectious.

As a man, you have a loving
and giving spirit, and a charm that
is unambiguous.

We are so proud of the
life you have made with
the love of your life.

We wish for you only
the best life has to offer,
for you always give your best.

Thirty candles on a birthday cake—
their light will soon extinguish, but
our love for you will burn forever.[5]

If I Could Save Time...

Time tore the innocence
from your heart,
left it bleeding playgrounds
and summer fun,
and I knew when I looked
into your eyes
you would never be my
little boy again.

The seasons are few
when our children
look to us for the answers
of life's mysteries,
those days now history,
the truth of our frailties
exposed under the stark
light of your growing up.

I want a do over, the chance
to hear your
little boy laugh once more,
the feel of your
little boy arms around my neck,
your warm, sweet breath
whispering in my ear, "Let me tell
you a 'swecret'."

I want to find the time that was lost
when the hour glass broke,
to reverse the tide of change
that swept you so far away.
I want you to be happy
but can no longer bear the cost,
shoulders stooped beneath the weight
of your absence.

I want you back again.

Has it been twenty-five years?

I thought her alive, resting
her eyes, hazel
with glints of gold.
They had seen eight
decades come and go,
pronounced each year
gone but not left behind.

I felt her absence before
I knew she was gone,
missed her presence
before I knew the separation
had even occurred.

I tasted the gulf that spans
the gap between here
and there. It was open
for a moment, just long enough
for her to cross over
but not long enough
for me to go with her.

I smelled the loneliness
of every day without her,
knowing life would never
be the same, not with the stench
of isolation in the air.

I heard the silence
where her laugh used to be,
a vacuum of harsh reality
that left me weeping,
crumpled on the floor
until I could think, feel, taste
smell and hear no more.

Contentment

the underside of the rainbow
is as cruddy
as a car in Pittsburgh

after four weeks of snow,

but the flip side of reality
is whatever
you want it to be.

I wanted you to know

before my words melt
down the drain
of nothingness

that if I could wear you

every day until there are
no more days
I would be content,

and that is my reality.

The Fine Art of Communication

She said, "You're driving me crazy,"
then with a laugh said, "I know, short
drive," and it was short, but not very
direct for she never quite made it to
the place called crazy, just the place
called haggard and annoyed.

He said, "Nothing I ever do is right."
She agreed, glad they could agree on
something, sorry it had to be that.
He took her agreement to mean
she acknowledged she was wrong,
she shouldn't be so critical. That was not

what she meant at all, but was it
worth the trouble to explain, to detail
what she really meant, and would he understand
it anyway? Didn't he really hear not
what she said, but what he wanted to hear?

Don't we all?

It's Always Something

In the immortal words of
Roseanne Roseannadanna,
"It's always something."

Your car is broken down
or you have to get a crown,
it's tax time again or you
haven't got a friend. It's
either too hot or it's stormy
weather, you and your sweetie
just can't get it together.

It's always something,
nothing is ever easy, enough
to make you queasy,
that life is all about change,
and change is usually
about something bad, or
at least something we dread.

When we were kids
life was simple, if things
were hard we didn't
know it, our parents
just didn't show it,
so we lived lives of
uncomplicated contentment,
never having reason
for worry or resentment,
but now we know
it's plain to see,
"It's always something,"
from birth to eternity.

Somewhere Over the Rainbow

He lives in La La Land, a place
where the sun is always shining
and you can never make more
than par on the golf courses.
There is nothing erratic in
his realm of fantasy, and the
only climactic thing that happens
are the few moments when he
is shaken from his stupor to
face the world as it is, not
as he would like it.

It is not a pretty sight.

Return to me

You are on so many pages
of my life, if I tried to
remove you the book
would look like a
brochure instead
of the volume
it really is.

Perhaps I failed
at letting you know
how vital you are to my
being, my existence a shadow
without you to laugh with, to share
things with. I should have been more
open to tell you how I felt.

I did not know.

Lessons are sometimes learned
too late, too late to make a
difference, too late to
prevent the minutes
and hours from
falling off the
clock and into

the ocean of no more time.

I look at you
in pictures and
sometimes I hear your
voice, but it is not enough,
not nearly enough.

Beacon of Light, Symbol of Culture

She never tires of seeing it, La Tour Eiffel
planted among the flowers on the left bank
of the Seine, comforted by the sameness

of its presence each time she visits,
the barren steel skeleton strangely solid
in a world that is fluid and ever changing.

Immediately recognizable many worlds
away, the tower glistens during the day
in the sun, but at night it is the sun, lighting

the sky, the walkways, the pulsating
strobes marking the top of each hour
until dawn, when it begins

its daily vigil again.

Lullaby
for Austin

Lullaby, close your eyes, as
the moon rises high from
the ground, let no sound
escape your lips, dream
my child of ports and ships,
sail away on moon beams
bright, and waken with
the morning light.

Caleb

Angelic face, sweet spirit
born into this world
eleven years ago while
we were still a thousand
miles away, enduring
the corporate life.

He loves playing games, videos,
Wii, but above all baseball--
pitching, outfielding, watching
and waiting for that perfect
ball that will connect
with his bat and end up

soaring over the back fence,
and we watch with pride
as he reaches home plate,
eyes bright, laughter
lifting the lowest state of mind,
and we are so thankful we have

a grandson named Caleb
as we watch him grow into
his name to become a man
of faith, devotion and sincerity.
Could anyone ask for anything
more?

Brad, Kenny and Rascal

It's a country song about an
old Ford truck, or maybe
someone has used up his
last bit of luck, or the

girl of your dreams is
here right beside you, or
maybe she's gone and
you don't know what to do.

You are either building bridges
or burning them down, living
in a big city or a one horse town.
It's those images of life that

Brad, Kenny and Rascal bring
when they turn up the volume
and begin to sing about things
familiar, things we all know about,

those songs of the country we
can't live without.

One Beet of your Heart

He paints forests with small, sable figures
pulling colossal vermillion hearts
through the snowy drifts

and we know that he knows
that love can ever survive
the starkest of environments,

the darkest of times.

We also know the painting
is authentic, not because
the gallery affirmed it,

but because Mackenzie Thorpe
is dyslectic, and the title "One
Beat of your Heart"

is spelled wrong.

A Winter's Tale

Winter crept in while I was all alone,
on the phone ordering pizza,
and I did not even know it was there,

did not hear its icy footfalls
or sense its dreary presence until
I felt its cold, unforgiving breath

upon my neck, and I turned
quickly to catch it in the act,
but it retreated outside before

I could grasp it, tell it I was
not ready, not yet, for fall
had only just begun, and I

was so enjoying the autumn sun.

Even the rocks cry out

Sun leaving its mark
on pallid land,
rain waiting for an
invitation but none
comes, and even
the stones seek shelter
from the overbearing
heat, praying for relief
but knowing
the rainmaker
is out of town.

Under the Banyan Tree

Twisted, tangled wood, magically
merging into one massive tree, branches

stretching, reaching, seeking to
cling together to form one unending

canopy, only green when viewed from above,
slightly eerie when encapsulated under

the emerald of the leaves amid
the grey of the gnarled, knotted trunks.

What a difference a day makes

Light falls down, tumbling down,
Jack and Jill don't make a sound,

water serves to cushion fall,
no sound is heard at all

as darkness yields its right to light
and dawn infringes on the night,

then the cycle begins again
and all is right in the sight of man.

Morning Light

Morning light, coming in bright
through my window, slow
to get up, get out of bed,
want to sleep in but too much
to do, so instead
I roll out, root about,
make coffee, feed Zoe,
and another day begins.

Honking Geese

Geese swimming above my head, honking
their way southward, currents in the air
carrying them to their destination,
a place where the table is set even in
winter, a transitory refuge for
all but the fragile few.

Sunset

The burnt orange clouds are tucked
into the horizon like a coverlet at
the foot of a bed, the vestigial
reminder of a sun that burned
hot and bright on this late
winter day in the South.

The Road to Happiness

Sun setting on another day, weary
but not undone, settling into
cushy chair, red wine in my
right hand, good book in
the other, nothing remains of the
day but a sliver of light on
the horizon, breathing in
peace, exhaling all things
that would steal my
tranquility. Ahhhh----

My Favorite Time of Year

Trees stir and kittens purr
and the coming night takes
a bite of a day soon gone,

yet we carry on,

taste of fall
lingering now,
in our mouths,

on our clothes,
apples cooking on the stove,
pies to bake, time to take

our leave as we sing autumn's song.

It's That Time of Year

The cumulus clouds become engorged
during the heat of the afternoon sun,
and now the cold air wrestles the
warm air to the ground, tries to pin it down
but it escapes, scales its way upward
and we are helpless spectators in
their life and death game.

The trees gyrate frenetically to the gusts
of wind, while birds hide within
the heaving branches, and I worry
about the bird's nest I saw just
the other day, when the sun
was shining and there was no portent
that storms were on the way.

Lightning hops, skips and jumps
almost playfully in the sky, but
we know better, we do not believe
the lie that there is no danger
as it calls to us, "Come out and play,
really, we won't hurt you, come
see our majestic display."

But we are not fooled, we have
lived too long in the South to
think thunderstorms benign,
so we shrink from the sight of
it, sink into a cubby hole hollowed
out in the closet, and wait it out,
just wait it out.

Cicada Time in Richmond

We heard them before we saw them,
the whirring of their mating song sounding
like a rotating lawn sprinkler, only much
louder, wondered at first the source
of the incessant drone, magnified
by the sheer numbers in the chorus
until it was really all you could hear.

They had emerged from their resting
place underground under cover
of darkness, seeking a mate and then
a nesting place, thousands upon
thousands of cicadas, their twelve
year cycle almost complete,
they clung tenaciously to the trees,
the shrubs, even to the window screens,
the sheen of their translucent wings
glistening in the morning sun.

That Explains A Lot

We have dogs.
We love our dogs, they are not pets
but part of the family. (We think the
oldest one is beginning to resemble
us.)

People ask why we don't travel more.
We have dogs.
Our time spent away from them is
never as enjoyable as our time
together.

People wonder why we do not
entertain more. We have lots of friends.
We have dogs.
Our dog family gets upset when we bring
strangers into the house.

We wonder if we have some recalcitrant
gene that puts us just outside of the circle
of normalcy and inside the prism of oddity.
We have dogs.
Our dogs are not animals, but people with feelings,
likes and dislikes.

You can only understand our devotion
if you, too, have dogs and then it does
not seem quite so aberrant when you invite
us over for several hours and we decline because...
we have dogs.

Rain Drops Keep Falling on my Head

Rain drops playing hopscotch
with arid ground, thunder

growling after being disturbed
from another afternoon nap,

wind snapping at the trees
and dogs swarming at my feet,

looking for refuge from yet
another Arkansas storm.

God's Blessings

Grandchildren are God's way of rewarding
you for the countless nights of worry, prayer
and faith that your children would be all right.

They are a priceless treasure, pure beyond measure
and you live for the sound of their laugh
and the touch of their hands upon your face.

Grandchildren remind you of what it was like
to be young and give your children a glimpse
into the sacrifices you willingly made for them.

The more you are blessed to be with them,
the more you want to be with them,
for life is never as complete as when they are near.

Grandchildren are a gift from God to prove
you still have something to give, a reason
to live, and the delight they have in your presence

is reciprocated one hundred fold, for when they
look in your eyes and say "Do it again, Grandpa,"
it is something that will never grow old.

Deaf in One Ear, Can Not Hear Out of the Other

The small box was tucked inside my mother's bra,
nestled safely between her breasts along with wires
winding their way up to her stone deaf tone deaf ears,
where sounds were magnified but not clarified,
so what was the point?

I exaggerated my words because she believed
she could read lips, a belief founded in fallacy.

Odd that the loss of that one sensory perception,
the ears' inability to conduct sound waves, would
effectively isolate her from so much and from so
many, yet lack of hearing went hand in hand
with lack of understanding,

rendering us unable to form the normal mother
daughter bond that depends on hearing and listening.

She was cheated out of a lifetime of aural experiences—
brooks, birds, baby's first words. I was robbed
of the closeness we should have had,
we deserved to have,
all because she was

deaf in one ear and could not hear
out of the other.

More than a Memory

Have you ever noticed
some memories are so strong
you can almost taste them,
almost smell them, almost feel
the touch of them
on your arm?

It is then that all of our
senses are suddenly engaged,
when the memories become
more vivid
than what we did today.
Even more important
is the way they make us feel,
more warm, more alive,
extraordinarily real,
for in the midst of daily living
too few memories are made,
too many things left undone,
too many words
left to say.

Part 2: Faith

Heart Attitude

Heart attitude, soul gratitude for
what I have, what I am able to do
for others, expecting, wanting

nothing in return, don't rob me
of my blessing, let me help you,
let me do for you what you

cannot do for yourself.
The example has been set,
all we must do is follow.

A woman's got to do what a woman's got to do

We are a circle of women,
         never-ending
because that's what circles are,
sometimes bending
because that's what women do.

Our willingness to compromise
         should not
be perceived as weakness,
because weak we never are
and fragile we will never be.

We were nice young girls
         who became
good, caring women
but who ultimately realized
nice girls don't change the world
and good women don't win the prize.

So we became dangerous women,
         women on the edge
of controversy, yet we are not controversial,
women with a vision for change,
yet we do not espouse change
for change's sake alone.

We lead busy lives, we wives,
          mothers,
widows, sisters, daughters,
we women who have formed a circle
of light and life, a circle
that will wrap all who enter
in arms of love and protection.

We are a circle of women,
          growing,
for our love touches one another
and reaches into each heart,
sowing kindness, reaping
the same, a circle of comfort,
the Mary Circle by name.

We lost a friend today

in memory of Dr. Gene Pynes, 4/18/2010

Gene was gentle, kind
and loving.

We lost a friend today.

Gene had a quirky sense
of humor,
always laughing at his own jokes.

We lost a comic today.

Gene had a penetrating vision
of the Scriptures,
inerrant in his understanding and depth.

We lost a scholar today.

Gene was a unique individual,
a man who studied hard, taught well,
and worked until the day he died.

We lost a role model today.

And today, even as we mourn,
we know, we are assured,
that Heaven gained a champion today.

Kindness

Why are we so critical of others, when
there is so much unfinished work
in our own lives?

How can we see the splinter in another's
eye when the log in our own eye obscures
our vision, or at least alters our perception?

Wouldn't it be remarkable if kindness
instead of criticism
seeped from every pore and settled
on the doorstep of each person we visited?

It's Friday but Sunday's Coming

It is in the darkest of the
midnight that we truly need
the light, something
we can use to find our
way, to lead us forward into
a day where we are free of trouble, free
of woes after we are dealt yet
another of life's blows.

What can we do, where can we turn
when we have no choice
in the events that churn
about us, leaving us heartsick
and dejected, what can be done
after we have objected to
life spinning out of control,
leaving only chaos and despair,
to whom can we go?

When the free will God gave us
is no longer free, but bends
to the will of others, where does
that leave you and me?

It's Friday but Sunday is coming
is the simple refrain that keeps rolling
over and over in my brain, so I grasp
tightly this hope that tomorrow will be
brighter and happier if we only believe
that God is the Author and Finisher of our
faith, that this, too, shall pass, this
heartache will eventually abate.

It's Friday, but Sunday is coming.

When we all get to Heaven

in memory of Dr. Bill Casey

A man of gentle spirit, uncommon valor,
his joy of living never waned
even as the minutes and days
stacked higher against the walls
of the hourglass.

He spoke of hope, ever optimistic,
his face mirrored the peace his soul felt
and he made us feel it, too,
made us believe he could beat
that dread disease.

The accolades and awards were many,
but one got the impression the prize
he yearned for had not yet been given,
the ceremony where he was the honoree
had not yet occurred.

But today he sits at the table of the King,
his face a shining reflection of the glory
in his midst, and we know he is saving
room at the table for each of us
when our race is run.

We are grateful to have known him,
thankful God allowed our paths to cross
even for a brief moment in time,
and we look forward to that great reunion,
the hope of all who believe.

Never Give Up

The staircase is curved and ornate.
From where I am standing it goes
up, but for one at the top, it comes
down, down to where I am, down

to where my feet meet that first
riser, and I grab the golden railing
as though it is the last thing I will
ever touch, ever hold, and I step,

step up to see what waits above,
beyond what I can comprehend, past
the mundane, superseding the ordinary,
my legs weary but my spirit strong

I pull my way to the top, where
I believe there is light and life,
I continue on, the steps endless
but the exhilaration real now as

I seek some unknown, unnamed
prize at the top of the stairs.

Feeding the Homeless

We broke bread with them,
the homeless who had been bused
in to our church in the suburbs,
far away from downtown shelters
and doorways closed to them
during the day, but at night
providing some protection
from the cruel elements
of winter.

I saw one man looking at me,
smiling
because I was laughing with
another man in the line, and I
looked away, embarrassed
that I was being scrutinized.

My actions caused the joy
to fall from his face,
his spirit crushed
and then I was the one awash
with regret that I made him feel bad.

That was ten years ago this
coming winter, and I still
wear the guilt like a
coat I no longer like,
but cannot throw away.

The Eleventh Hour

Even in my darkest hour, I still hope.
Even in my most hopeless state,
I still pray. Especially in my

most hopeless state, for it is
then that I must rely on Him
who has the answers that

I crave, and if He chooses
not to give me what I seek,
I am confident He will

at least give me what I need,
a time of solace, a brief respite
from the worries of this world.

Even in my darkest hour, I still hope.
Even in my most hopeless state,
I still pray.

Lord, Hear our Prayer

Each day some new tragedy,
too much to bear
we need blessed relief,

a fresh new rain
poured down from heaven
to give us a reprieve

from pain, heartache,
too much to bear,
where is the answer,

does anyone care
that lives are shattered,
broken beyond repair?

Lord, hear our prayer,
Lord, hear our prayer.

A Righteous Man

In memory of Hermon Galloway

Isa 7:9 If you do not stand firm in your faith, you will not stand at all.

Isaiah 40:30-31. 30 Even youths grow tired and weary, and young men stumble and fall; 31 but those who hope in the Lord will renew their strength. They will soar on wings like eagles; they will run and not grow weary, they will walk and not be faint.

With faith and strength
he lived his life,
a long life,
a good life,
a life of quiet fortitude.

He was a godly man.

During World War II
he took the oath to
serve and protect,
training others
to do the same.

He was a godly man.

Keeping covenant with his wife,
with his God,
with his employer,
raising his children
with integrity to have integrity.

He was a godly man.

Now he has made the transition
from earth to heaven,
his spirit joyous,
his body at rest,
his mission on earth completed at last.

He was a godly man, a righteous man,
a man who will not soon be forgotten.

Next year in Jerusalem

Next year in Jerusalem, a phrase rendered
archaic by some, volatile by others,
are to me words of hope, words of redemption,
words reminding us of that New Jerusalem
to come.

I am not Jewish, but my Redeemer is.
I am not planning on moving to Jerusalem,
but my Redeemer is.
I am not seeking that which cannot be found,
or He who will not return again,
for my Redeemer is readily found
and He will, indeed,
return again.

Next year in Jerusalem, the hope
of all who believe, the reality
of all who know the redemptive
love and grace of Jesus,
the Christ.

I know my Redeemer lives.
I know my Redeemer has already begun
His journey back to Jerusalem.
I know I am ready.
I know.[6]

Hope for tomorrow

When there is only the scream
of a person dying within you,
when your sighs are not of contentment

but exasperation, when you know
not the joy of life but
the drudgery of living,

when days go from bad to worse,
where do you go from there?

It is then that you need hope
for tomorrow and peace
for today--it passes understanding,

you know. There is a way out,
He says--it is a narrow path
but one you must traverse.

It is the new birth that gives worth
to lives no longer worth living.

It is grace carried on the back of faith,
delivered through penitent prayer.
Hope is born there, prayer resides there,
and faith comes into maturity there.

Two hundred feet ahead

Ribbon of road stretches
toward tomorrow, night
looms larger, vision
impaired, but car
lights illumine
the path
before me, and
I can see clearly
two hundred feet ahead.

Ribbon of life stretches
toward the unknown,
precarious, ever
changing, vision
impaired, but
God delivers
me through
the dark shadows,
for He can see clearly
the pitfalls ahead.

If I can depend on car
lights to transport me
over potholes and around
the next bend, how much more
can I depend on my Savior,
whose vision is limitless,
whose love never ends.

God is always with me
of that I am sure,
the need to know
unimportant,
the need to see,
petty now. Faith's
headlights shine the way
before me, and I am
two hundred feet closer now.

The Power Behind the Word

Words can be billowy gauze
wrapping the listener in softness
and comfort.

They can be as familiar as the
old blanket covering you
on a cold winter's night,
or as foreign as someone
babbling in unknown tongues.

But words can also be arrows
dipped in poison, wounding without
discrimination, fatal in their attraction.

Words can be fulfilling, but they can
also cause anger and hurt to come
spilling out of your heart and onto the
person closest to you.

Hearing the spoken word (if you
have hearing) is not optional, but
listening is.

Heeding the spoken word renders
you some choice—will you or will
you not be obedient to its call, give
credence to its message?

I choose to accept those words
that give life and reject wholeheartedly
those words that would rob me of life,
liberty and the pursuit of all things
happy. For I know, I truly understand,
the power behind the word.

A Glimpse into Heaven

In memory of Charles Cromley

Faith is the substance of things hoped for,
the evidence of things not seen.
Heb 11:1

When we at last reach the end
of this temporal existence,
and the beginning of a new
reality somewhere in the distance,
the lines between the two
are sometimes blurred.

He had lain there for days,
unable to say good-bye,
unaware of family, friends,
until abruptly he had eyes
that could see and ears
that could hear

and with a voice strong and clear
sang out, "Oh what a foretaste
of glory divine." At a time
when life flowed from him
in dribs and drabs, he was given
a gift, a blessed assurance

of that life to come. And his family,
faithful and loving, shared
in that gift, receiving the tangible
evidence of things not yet seen
through the eyes and ears of one
given a glimpse of heaven.

All About Faith

I claim to have faith, and indeed
I do have the faith to believe,
but do I have the faith to live?

I believe there is one God
who took chaos and made it
orderly.

I believe in Jesus Christ,
who took the mayhem of my life
and made it amenable.

I believe in the Holy Spirit
who guides me through darkness
and into the coming light.

But where is my faith
when I am maligned,
misunderstood, abused?

Where is my willingness
to suffer all for the cause
of Jesus Christ?

I need to plant the seed
of faith and nourish it daily
with prayer and God's Word.

I need water walking faith,
not just sweet talking faith
to make it through another day.

Faith, substance, hope,
and evidence, if not seen
must be experienced.

The faith of a child, the evidence
of the wild thing made tame,
the substance of belief.

That is what this thing called
faith is all about.

...and your sons and your daughters will prophesy

Joel 2:28
for Michael, our hero

He has eyes that have seen no evil,
lips that have spoken no guile,
ears that hear whispers of angels
and a spirit undefiled
by the cares and concerns of a fallen world,

he is deaf to the siren's call,
but he hears loudly and clearly
the sound of our Savior
and eagerly awaits the small,
still voice that beckons him to be faithful
and follow closely behind,

so that he won't miss a word of comfort
or fail to see the Son shine
on that day of His appearing,
his heart won't skip a beat
when he hears the call
"Come home, my child,
and sit at the Master's feet."

I hear a rumble.

He has no need for fortune or fame,
he is one of the innocent few
chosen by God to speak His name
and to share with all the Good News.
Jesus is coming.

I hear a rumble, Jesus is coming,
listen, and you can hear it, too.
God would not tell me if it were not so,
get ready, get ready to go.

I'm so happy.

I hear a rumble, Jesus is coming, I'm so happy.

For Such a Time as This

Events orchestrated, coincidences
occur that leave us
scratching our heads in wonder,
reeling from the thunder
of what could have been, what should
have been another ill defeat,
yet God was in the details
and the victory was sweet
because He raised up another
warrior for such a time as this,
and again we saw His saving
grace, the evidence that He exists.

God is raising up warriors
all across the land,
mighty in His strength
but how can they withstand
the march of Satan's army
growing day by day,
and the hopelessness and futility
that seem to darken our way?
Even many churches
have floundered and gone to sleep,
while God's children are beaten and bruised
and thrown upon the heap.

God is raising up warriors
for such a time as this,
when we must rely upon the One
with the nail scars in His wrist.
Can you hear God calling
your name out loud and clear,
can you step out from the shadows
and throw off the cloak of fear?

Many will be chosen
but only some will heed the call
to follow the Master where he leads,
to willingly give their all.

Who knows, perhaps you have been chosen
for such a time as this.[7]

Don't Cry for Me

In memory of Darrell Dover

When the slender thread that ties
me to this earth is severed,
my soul finally will be free
and when I am untethered

I will reach heights that until now
had been beyond my grasp,
and surrounded by the light of God
I know that I will clasp

the hand of Jesus as my loved
ones wait to greet me.
I will walk among those gone before
as all of Heaven turns out to meet me.

I know you will miss my presence,
and I will miss you, too.
Do not be sad and forlorn, my love,
I will be reunited with you.

But until God is ready to call for you
and your face again I see,
know that I am finally home,
my dear, don't cry for me.

The Last Word

Thorny words that pricked my pride,
left me bleeding resentment
and wanting to blame,

I slung fiery arrows
left nothing inside.
Hurling accusations

I did not even take aim,
just pulled the trigger
and let my words scatter.

The avalanche that resulted
killed and maimed
not just those who had hurt me

but the innocent were shattered.

How could I be so thoughtless,
so what if I was insulted?
We need to learn once and for all,

we need to finally answer the call
to stop being heartless
to put others first,

then Kingdom living will finally take hold
and Kingdom understanding
will rule over all.

On the Jericho Road

Pathway hewn from limestone,
thread-like, barren, and bare,
mirrors my soul when I stray
from the place God wants me to be.

Life is a series of choices,
distractions must not lead the way.
I must focus now on hope,
peace and love, I must forever

stay on the path that's called holy,
to wander never again,
seek out the wisdom of the ages,
pray until my journey's conclusion

and allow God's spirit to lead me
higher and higher each day,
until I reach the peak of the mountain
called Faith, until I finally see God's face,

there on the Jericho Road.

Perfected in Love

Surrounded by so great a cloud of witnesses
we press forward, toward the high calling,
seeking the state of holiness, sanctified
for God's own purpose.

The path, not always even, is well worn
and well marked. The faithful
always leave signposts to help
the newly born on his way.

After years spent on the same walkway,
the path begins to smooth—grace
does that.

The things we used to struggle against
now distant memories as we fix
our eyes on the prize, the long ago gift
of salvation now a dazzling reminder

of the love poured out for us on Calvary,
the love that saved us, that set us apart,
that perfected us so that we, too,
can offer a sacrificial love to all

we meet along the way. Not perfect
in body, soul or thinking, but spirit so
intertwined

with our Father that love now reigns
supreme, and we leave grace gifts
wherever we go, knowing salvation
is not some far away, unattainable

entity, but it is here, it is now, present
in everything we say and do. It is
all grace.

Part Three:
This Writing Life

The Writer's Pen

Since I have started writing again,
I issue this warning to family and friends--
everything is fodder for the writer's pen.

But What Does it Mean to You?

I go to my Creative Writing class
and flinch as my peers try to flog
the truth out of each poem,

desperately attempting to force
the meaning into a tiny square
shape, even though the gist

may be round to some,
or triangular to others,
but they will not rest

until it is neatly packaged
and wrapped up
with a bow.

Wouldn't it be Great

Wouldn't it be great to have a poem
in which you included all of your
favorite words, like coalesce
and condescend, visceral and
effervescent, words that would
be the essence of what you love
about words, and that would
bring you back again to
ruminate upon their meanings,
to enlighten and illuminate,
and then further envision the shape,
the size, the feel that each word makes?

It is not just the meaning that
gives me pause, it is the sound
of each word that soothes or claws
its way into my very soul,
the way the words feel as they roll
off my tongue and onto the page,
where the image becomes
the thought, and the thought
the word, and the word engages
my mind to begin the process
all over again.

River of Words

The rock was from the river bed
of the Buffalo, worn smooth and
round by the water's endless caress
at that spot where the depth was
only three feet and the warmth
was like a soothing bath.

The words I explore each day
wear my tongue smooth from
the way they pour from my
soul onto the page, and even
when they choose to trickle
they tickle my teeth,

and I luxuriate in their presence,
the warmth of their company
comforting me in my solitude,
caressing me in a crowd,
and somewhere in the distance
I hear water polishing stone.

Where Have All the Poems Gone?

I have not found great poetry
written on bathroom walls,
but do not doubt it could happen.

I have found I must seek out
poetry, search for it as one
divining for that last drop
of water from a river bed wrung dry,

not because good poetry is not
abundant nor because it plays
hide and seek with those who
long for its form, but because

good poetry is not quickly
rewarded in this era
of MTV and text messaging
when words are altered

to a semblance I can no longer
recognize, and poems are
deconstructed to fit
on a two inch screen.

I Am A Poet

Going over words on paper
or the computer
for the thousandth time,
revision or new vision,
which shall it be?

I am a storyteller, the genre
as important as the tales
I tell, the shape of the words
as vital as the feelings
they elicit.

Gathering together words
to make a collection,
my husband says, "Why
not write something that sells--
how about fiction?"

I am a poet, the words
carefully chosen, not
some hash hastily thrown
together nor a formula
dutifully followed

so that only the names
change, but every
scene remains the same,
and every conclusion
a ready resolution.
I am a storyteller, a poet,
and life is reduced to exist
on twenty pound paper
between soft covers held together
by the glue of passion and observation.

Riding the Rails

If I speak of things that cause me pain
people tune out, not eager to hear
me whine about my life and all
of its disappointments.

But if I write the same things down,
commit them to paper and transform them
into a poem, for some inexplicable
reason they begin to carry some weight.

Poetry, therefore, becomes my means
of communicating with the world,
whether sharing my joy or exposing
my pain, poetry is my mode of transportation,

the train I take to ride out my journey
of self discovery and oftentimes healing,
the path straightened out by the rails
upon which I ride, the bumps and hills

of my life softened by the mechanical
devices that keep my train solidly on its
track, whether using alliteration or rhyme,
my train rambles on to its destination

and I ride comfortably, knowing that
when I reach my journey's end I will
have my poems to comfort me, and you,
the readers, will be my new best friends.

The Morning Hours

I get up in the early morning hours,
and after attending to the dogs
turn on the computer and fill

my plate full of words. I leave long
enough to make the coffee, half caffeine
and half decaf, and bring back

the steaming brew to the room
that houses my computer, hoping
I will get a jump on a day that is certain

to impede my writing. Sure enough,
time jostles my arm, the plate is upended
and the words fall heavily onto my desk,

not in any particular order,
and I am left
to clean up the mess.

The Ten Poem Rule

I write ten poems in an effort
to bring one poem to fruition, for
this is how it goes.

Three poems will be adequate
and I can use them as filler in a
collection.

Three poems will be good,
and I will use them as signposts
to show others the way.

Three poems will be ill conceived,
and they will never see
the light of day.

But one poem will undoubtedly
become the best poem I have
ever written, one poem

out of ten will confirm
that I am a poet, I can
string words together

to form that combination
of sights and sounds, feelings
and observations that, if I have

done my job, will seep into
your consciousness, shining a light
of truth upon your path, bringing out

feelings you did not know you had,
for I write not to show you my life,
but to show you yours.

The Graveyard of Lost Words

One word follows obediently after another
until they march across the page, carrying
crumbs of thought upon their backs,
stray thoughts left behind
as I clumsily write down
what is on my mind.

Or, sometimes the words congregate
to sing praise of alliteration or
assonance, and occasionally
even rhyme--the appearance,
the sound syllables make
elicit their reverence.

I see the words floating about my head
like animated words from vocabulary
lessons so many years ago, now
searching, seeking for a place
to stay, a place where they
can hide away.

And I have that place, right here
in my computer's memory, a
place where words are safe,
a refuge for the stragglers
and ill conceived, a home
where they will find reprieve.

The words still echo in my mind
like faded images left behind
when everything is said
and done, and nothing
remains, nothing
remains.

But it really happened that way

As a novice to poetry, I began
by writing poems that included
each and every detail of important
events in my life. Each and
every detail.

My professor pointed out
that to write good poetry,
one must be concise,
make every word count.
"But it really happened that way,"
I retorted, to which he simply
smiled, not resorting to
enlighten me on how many
times he had heard that phrase.
Professor Burns did not teach
by making us feel bad about
our lack of writing skills, but by
instructing us how we could do
better, "Show, don't tell."

I now understand what he
tried to say--poetry must
be true without getting in the
way of what we feel when we hear
it, what it inspires us to do.
We must be true to the poem
and what it conveys,
save the facts for another day.

It really happened that way.

The Word Dance

Fever spikes like pitchforks
and words flit before my eyes
like grazing butterflies

and I reach out and grab
a verb and a noun
and a dangling

participle, and then I
arrange them in a manner
that makes sense, at least to me,

and the words are a cold cloth
pressed against the fire
that is my forehead

and I lay my head
down to rest, arms too
heavy to reach for more anyway.

Writing what you know

The poet wrote about alcoholism,
his personal battle, and the reader
asked, "Why would you write
about that?"

"That's what poetry is," replied
the poet. "It is bits and pieces
of our lives, dissected and examined,
displayed for

all to see." And so it is. Fragments
of what we have lived, done, seen,
all splayed out on the autopsy table
waiting for

the examiner's knife, cutting through
to the heart of who we are, what
we have experienced, still searching
for the why.

This Writing Life

I walk the street straight, avoiding the curves
and always making right turns until I am back
again, where I began, my leisurely stroll
not meant for exercise or anything quite so
positive, but designed for one purpose only,
to rescue me from the keyboard
so I can live life,
and not just write about it.

I live my life straight, avoiding the curves
fate tosses out, trying to make right choices
if I have a choice, but ending up where I
started, not on the same street but
the same town, and the town has
changed, but so have I, so I look
around, gather more fuel for whatever
I am working on, and just write,

for the streets may change,
but this process of writing
remains the same.

As the Words Turn

I read other poets, not to steal their words
or ideas, but to get a feel for the way
the words turn, the pirouettes
that send them spinning
into new directions, new frontiers,
and I am delighted at Richard Jones' exploration

of solitude in "White Towels," tickled
by Billy Collins rendering of "Another reason
why I don't keep a gun in the house" (I can
seldom recall the title, so it is just "Barking Dogs"
to me) and I think if I read enough, I will surely absorb
ample inspiration so that my poems, too, will

send the reader on an expedition of new horizons found,
if I can only find a pen filled with liquid soul still willing
to spill its life out onto the blank page, a perfect sacrifice
for just one more day, one more hour, one more poem.

Waiting For the Poem

I should be folding towels, straightening
up the house, but here I am writing
yet another poem, this one about
why I should be doing something
other than writing a poem.

If I stared at my reflection in a pond
until I wasted away to nothing
it would make more sense than writing
about why I should not be writing.

Even my dogs hate my laptop and wonder
if it tastes better than it looks.
Barking accompanies each keystroke
because my attention is diverted
from them, my canine family,
and after all, it is all about them.

But for this moment, this episode in the life
of a poet, it is not all about them, but instead
it is all about the poem, the shape
of it, the feel of it, the weight
of it, the wait for it.

Part Four:
Left, Right, or In Between

Choices

Slave or free,
free or oppressed,
oppressed or liberated,
where do you stand?

Do you stand for freedom
as long as those set free
do not impact you?
Do you rail against oppression

only if you are the oppressed?

Do you ring the bell
for liberty so that all may hear its sound?
Or, do you silence it with your voice
or with your vote, thinking, believing

not all are created equal,
there are inferior races
and not all deserve to benefit
from Maslow's hierarchy of needs?

How do you reconcile
slavery to a child?
How do you justify
your freedom while others

are oppressed?
How do you keep silent
when your voice,
joined with others,

could create a concert choir
of freedom that could
sing to change the world?
When will you stand

and be counted
among those
who are willing to fight
for basic human rights

for basically every human?

When will you honor God
by honoring man,
by validating His plan
that whoever helps

the least among us is
truly helping, truly serving,
truly worshipping
God?

Where do you stand?

Where *do* you stand?

Where do *you* stand?

1961

Leaving downtown Little Rock after
a day of shopping, paying bills,
boarded bus to Fair Park, Mama,
Cheryl, and me. 1961, bus was full
and hot.

An elderly woman, hair frosty
with small, black hat perched
atop her head stood and held onto the pole,
drained of energy, devoid of hope
she held onto the pole.

I was ten—I offered her my seat,
she looked away, Mama scolded.
They knew the rules,
I did not.

A Hill of Beans

A hill of beans, something
I have never seen
but nevertheless understand.

It is the proclivity to view
out of proportion
those things inconsequential

> *while ignoring the essential.*
> *Does a Mayfly focus on the fleeting events,*
> *major on the minor,*

or does he make the most
of his 24 hours, knowing
the margin of error is so slight

> *there is no room for mistake?*

Can we learn from the Mayfly,
or is our mindset so firmly fixed
we can no longer take on knowledge

but instead let any new thought
pour out of us as through a sieve,
losing one idea at a time until

> *there is no new thinking, no new resolve.*

A Young Woman Remembered
for Neda[8]

Spirit sings a song of freedom,
but song cannot escape lips
silenced,

a human sacrifice is offered
to the gods of depravity
and death.

Her life now carved in linear fashion
upon the roads where her blood
is spilled,

down the alleyways to reach another
who would dare chant of peace, a dream
to chase.

Should not angels guard our presence,
remind our Lord of our existence?
We taste

the saltiness of a mother's tears.
The one who stole your future away
surely

has a mother, too, whose visage will
one day be distorted as tears blend
with mud

and blood and human waste until
a terrorist has a face and all who wreak
havoc

upon our world will lose their place,
their sovereign reign deposed
at last.

The demon exposed, the blind can
see, and hate is put to death for
eternity.

Changing the world is easier said than done

We were the generation born
after World War Two, so many
babies, they called it a boom,
and we wore our hope like a badge
pinned tightly to our vest, the assurance
that we could right all wrongs
because our nation was blessed.

We set our faces like flint and our
shoulders firmly against the stone,
and we worked to keep our nation great
and to make our feelings known.
We worked when we felt mad,
we worked when we were sad,
we worked when things looked bad,
and we worked until we had
nothing else to do, but did not know
we had no real control,
we might as well have worn our bobby sox
and just played rock and roll.
The government held the power
and we learned too late that the hour
of our discontent had passed,
all of our money and time and effort
was not enough to last and so we owe you,
our children and our grandchildren,
the greatest apology of all.

We were going to change the world,
but the world changed us instead,
we were going to save the world
but that notion was put to bed
so we bow out quietly, nothing left to do,
but send our regards to Broadway
and give our regrets to you.

Malice in Wonderland

The looking glass is not so clear
as it was even at this time last year.
The world events were getting squirrely
and even Alice thought that surely

her adventure in Wonderland
would soon come to an end.
Yet here we are in some strange world
groping for stability, hoping for civility

as the wizards of Wall Street
can no longer stand the heat
and the politics of want more power
are now the bywords of the hour.

The malice in Wonderland makes me ill,
and sometimes I think I took the wrong pill.
I should have swallowed whole the one that let me sleep,
would have been better off if I could keep

the knowledge of who we are closed up in a jar
and who we will be hidden from me.
How can we salvage the remnants of good
when scavengers pick the bones dry and bathe in the blood

of the innocent bystander, what hope is there now
to leave our children better off, somehow?
I strain to reach the light switch to turn off the dark,
but hope puddles around me, reality too stark.

That's just the way it was

Things have changed in the world.

When I was a child, scores were counted
and one side won, one side lost--
that's just the way it was.

When I was a teen, grades were counted
and honor rolls were made or missed--
that's just the way it was.

When I became an adult, days off were counted
and too many days missed meant the lack of a raise--
that's just the way it was.

Until this year I thought the Nobel Prize was awarded
for excellence achieved, not dreams conceived--
        I thought praise was reserved for good that was done, not
good that was undone--
        I thought honor was given for bravery on the front, not
cowardice in the back rooms of Congress--
        I thought unity was the backbone of America, and trusting
in God was the foundation--
when did these things change?

When I am old, much older than today,
I hope my grandchildren and nieces and nephews
can say I stood up
for right and faced evil in the eye--

        that's just the way it was.

All Roads Lead to Rome

Counting nines, counting twelves
counting monkeys on the shelves.
Change, frightening to behold
yet no new stories to be told.

Life goes on the way it must
but if it doesn't, it's only dust.
What was created is now torn down,
monkeys scattered all around.

We once used money to light the fires
as we sought and bought our heart's desires.
The money tree has lost its limbs
and now we rock and sing our hymns.

Amazing grace is all that's left,
security gone, we are bereft
and monkey see, monkey do
has not worked out for me or you.

Economy imploded, culture shocked
to see the fragility when Wall Street rocked.
The cycle of greed almost complete,
no one left standing on his feet.

Hear no evil, speak or see,
the monkey down on bended knee
praying to his gods above,
put away their boxing gloves.

And to the God upon His throne
we pray escape from the fate of Rome.
A once great empire rose and fell,
we hear the toll of that same bell.

Monkey see, monkey do,
if only we had learned from you.

An Ode to my Democratic friends
for John, Betty Jo, Val and Rhona

Can Republicans and Democrats be friends
or do politics preclude such ends?
Do your friends' ideals draw ire
or can you overlook the political fire?

Is there such a thing as a yellow-dog Republican?
Aren't we all really just Americans?
I admit it is hard for me to comprehend
the choices of such good friends.

But I know they have confusion, too,
when then see me vote red instead of blue.
In the end I give thanks to our Lord
that we can all unite in one accord

if not at the polls at least at church
where neither party is left in the lurch.
We are all children of an awesome God
with no need to put up a phony facade.

And thanks to America we each still have a vote
and we are all so well-bred we would never gloat
when one party, either red or blue, comes out ahead,
but be assured, when Republicans lose,

I will always bleed red.

Atlas Shrugged

The earth tilted and Atlas shrugged
convinced he had the strength,
could go to any length
to hold the world upright.

The entire earth rumbled,
geography tumbled
as mountains fell to the seas
and no help was in sight.

Humanity cringed,
the earth was singed
with the fires of judgment
and cries into the night.

The earth grew tired
and humanity was mired
in misery and pain
and wrong picks over right.

The earth righted
and Atlas shrugged convinced
his job was done at last,
he pulled the cord, turned off the light.

Ribbon of Death

I never felt the desperation
that ends only with a bullet.

As the brownish orange sludge slinks in to colonize
the ceramic beaches, more than nature
is brought to its knees, more than
a needed resource is lost.

Tracks of salt mar our faces as we witness pelicans
carpeted in something never meant
to mix with water, a cliche
born from truth.

Yet, here it is, even now an orange ribbon, unrelenting,
sinister in its intent, reminding
everyone in its path that life
and livelihoods

are too fragile to balance on the wall,
unable to withstand the fall

and one man could no longer shoulder the reality
that the life he built was over,
so when the ribbon came
the bullet came with it.

Part Five:
What's left to say?

Waiting....

Sometimes I like to hide in plain sight,
hold my breath and count to ten, waiting
for someone, anyone, to Red Rover me over,

and then

sometimes I am the snake who swallowed
its own tail, and I am safe and warm in my
own dark space until I regurgitate myself
back into the light,

and then

I seek out the nearest stone under which
I can hide until I hear the magic words,
"Simon Says slink to the center."

And then

I slide out from under my secret place
only to see my reflection in a discarded
mirror and I am not a snake after all,
but a frog wearing a crown,

waiting...

Bridges

Random thoughts skim the surface of my brain
darting here and there like a pinball in a machine
slamming one memory, then being deflected

into another, totally unrelated event,
and this continues until I find myself
dizzy and confused, and I am

left wondering what sparks such strange
synaptic happenings—too many bridges
torched or not enough crossed?

Not yet, please not yet

I saw them outside the window
of Starbucks, and I knew
in an instant
they had been touched
by death.
Not a grazing touch,
not just a brushed shoulder
in passing, but an intimate
touch that would never
be forgotten.

The young girl had been
in front of me in line,
and I heard her order
café au lait with
a lilt in her voice,
no inkling
of what was to come.

The older girl came
to the door, called
her outside and there
it played out, their
story like frames
in a silent movie,
with no sound
or even captions,
but none was needed
as I saw the young girl's
body fold into her sister's,
and they both dropped
to the ground, the sidewalk
pulling them down
until the cold, grey
cement was all they could feel,
all they wanted to feel.

Ebb Tide
for Twila

The day had stretched on like
the highway that never ends.
Too depleted to even eat,
but then the music grabbed

her feet and she danced—
she danced with energy
she did not know she had,
she danced the day's hurts

away, and soon he joined
in and the fatigue sloughed
off and before the last song
ended they fell into each other's

arms, melded into one strong
union and knowing this moment
could never be exactly replicated
they vowed to remember

this night always, to keep
it tucked away in the safest
of places, so that when they
next found themselves

too tired to move, too tired
to eat, they would take out
the memory of the night
the music grabbed their feet.

The Twelfth of Never

The commercial features
an older woman and man.

Hand in hand they
walk a wooded path,
a younger couple behind them,
passing them, can't resist looking back,
casting glances at the couple
one more time. Hopeful
that the flower of their love will live
long enough to grow into a garden
with blossoms intertwined,
so that someday they will be the
older couple giving inspiration to
a newly found devotion.

The commercial is selling diamonds.
The thought is worth so much more.

No Greater Love

for Aldo Rubio
No greater love than to give your life for another... John 15:13

Little boy hero awoke that morning
with nothing but play on his mind,
went out with three good friends

not knowing how the day would end.

Did he tell his mother he loved her
before he walked through the door
or was he too busy, distracted,

his focus on friends exacted

the need to leave in haste, to speed
toward his destiny that would inextricably
alter the lives of friends and family

forever?

His friend, falling like a star from the sky
into a body of water threatening
to extinguish his light

yet young Aldo plunged in, ready to fight

for the life of the one in distress--
thinking he could make a difference,
and just as the waters released

one young boy, hope ceased

for Aldo as death's fingers wrapped
around his legs, pulled him downward,
downward to his final end,

what a true and loyal friend.

Then the angels lifted him upward, upward
to the heavenly heights, where he is hailed
as a hero of divine proportions

for no greater love has been apportioned

and though his parents and friends
will mourn his loss,
his life was not lost, but eternity found.

Walking with a purpose

I walk the path backwards
hoping to run into that
younger version of me,
wanting to explore her
face, free of wrinkles,
her eyes still bright
with the knowledge
that she has many more
tomorrows.

I come to the crossroad,
that place where choices
must be made, and can
no longer remember
which way I turned
to end up here. Would
I have done it differently
anyway?

I trip over my good
intentions and find
myself face down in
a puddle of indecision.
I linger like a swine
who is finally home,
but then remember
this is not my home, I
am better than this.

I lift my face to the
sky and am gratified
that a light, cleansing
rain washes me
fresh and then I am

off again, walking
the road straight, straight
to who I will be tomorrow.
Perhaps I will encounter her
yet, that younger, more hopeful
version of me. Will she listen if I tell
her what lies ahead?

Would you?

Come Sail Away with Me

She feels as though she is sailing
in a boat that is in danger of
reaching the end of the ocean,

breaching that part of the world
that is no more, and if she continues
she will fall, fall off the edge

into a world that is part make-believe
and part reality, where the lines
blur and the mind stirs

with echoes of the past
and whispers of the future.

Survivor

for Hildegard Sherman

Brave heart, pure heart,
escaping the stain on humanity
called the Holocaust,

still one more plan designed
by the enemy to eradicate
God's chosen, perpetrated

by one evil man, a man
with no soul who could so easily erase
six million mortals

and whose only regret
was the failure to achieve
his final solution.

One young girl
with blond locks and Aryan looks
whose stepmother stepped up

to shield an innocent
from certain demise
still remembers,

carries the scars of
a vile time when "trust no one"
was not a slogan

from a television show,
but a way of life
if you were to live.

Brave heart, survivor's heart
with stories still to tell--
tell them now.

Take a deep breath

Breathing does not come easily,
and I wonder why it comes
at all, if it begrudges the
expectation of its arrival.

It should be thrilled
someone is looking
forward to that next
breath, but instead

it holds on to it like
it is the last of its
kind, unwilling to
part with it, making

lips turn blue awaiting
the oxygen that fuels
the heart, greedy
in the way it holds

the next breath in
its tight little fists,
and I wonder why
God gave it so

much power, why
it controls life and
death, that tedious
thing called Breath.

Beware the monkey's paw

Star light, star bright, first star
I see tonight, wish I may....

If stars really granted wishes
even first stars, would
the world be different?

If candles on a birthday cake,
duly blown out in one, big
breath gave us our birthday
wish, would we be
different?

If wishes were horses, would
beggars really ride?

If we wished upon a falling star,
would our dreams come true,
or would we be destroyed
by a meteor?

A New Twist on an Old Tale

There was an old woman.
She had a husband but
he left her with a shoe

full of kids. She didn't know
what to do with them since
in this enlightened age

people no longer spank
their children and put them
to bed. So she just let

them have the run of the
Nike while she sat on
the porch solving Sudokus.

Here's to Progress

I still recall the sound of the train
rolling down the track, clickety-clack,
clickety-clack, the smoke from the stack
the only thing looking back

as it curled toward us, reaching out
for us, wanting us to remember it was
there, and the groaning of the cars
as they clutched those iron rails,

and of course the moaning of the whistle,
sweet and low and going on forever,
singing out the announcement of its
arrival. But what I waited for was

the caboose, always red, always bringing
up the rear, always inhabited by the conductor,
a man wearing a blue and white striped cap
and a smile and a wave, until one day

the caboose was deemed irrelevant,
and now there are generations
who will never experience the joy and elation
of the little red car pulling into the station.

Best Laid Plans

She intends to get up early, read
her Bible, do some deep breathing
while manipulating her body
into unnatural and sometimes
painful
positions, all in the name of
good health.

What actually happens is she
almost falls out of bed and onto
the floor, tripping over dogs and
toys and rushing to turn off the
alarm,
all to get the puppy outside
to avoid an accident.

She lives in a paradox, loving
people but cherishing her time
alone, and then resenting the
isolation that encases her like a
burial
shroud. She needs to get out, do
something, anything.

She remembers being a child,
running outside in the early
morning hours to feel the dew
on her bare feet, the smell of
rain
clogging the air, and she ran--
she ran, as though her

feet had wings and she
wondered if she could fly, felt
like at any moment she could
take to the sky, and then
her life
would really begin.

She intends to get up early, but
instead, just stays in bed.

Take it to the limits, **One More Time**

Aging band, graying fans
checking into Hotel California
       one more time.

Swaying to treasured tunes,
singing enduring lyrics,
youth resurrected
       one more time.

Dancing spotlights, images
cast upon a screen
enhancing the music,
falling head first into the rhythm,
       one more time.

Guitar riffs taste good in our mouths,
washing them down with words
so sweet, screaming our support
until voices can no longer
eclipse the volume,
       one more time.

Decades gone, vanished
in the dark as the Eagles
soar to new heights
and we go right along
with them, coaxing them upward,
leaving with a peaceful, easy feeling,
       one more time.

Defining Moments

The boy stands on the edge of manhood,
eager to cross the threshold but fearful
nonetheless,
for the shrillness of the moment
makes him shy away.
He calls for his mother but she is not there.

The light is too bright, creating
black stars in his eyes as he blinks
against the radiance meant to show
the way, but instead makes him turn
away, shielding his eyes from all he sees.

If he goes back he can crawl into his
bed, hide under the covers, and he
will be safe, but if he goes back, can
he ever return again to this moment,
to this defining time in his life?

Intuitively he knows he can not,
so he forages through his fears,
casting his net onto the waters
of his insecurity, and he will
do it again and again, until
he can stand brave and strong
for that is what men do.

A Change of Place

Chasing the air that escapes my mouth
I find myself in a different part of the city,
a place I have never been before,
and I can smell the indifference
and taste the solitude.

A swirl of thought ribbons around my head
that I recognize as regret, a desire to turn
back before it is too late, the blacktop
shimmering under the layer of ice
and the street signs wavering

in the wind, but I have waded too far in,
no one to life preserve me out of here,
(would they if they could)? Sucking
the frigid air into my lungs,
the coldness burns

leaving a raw taste in a mouth gone dry.
Cannot swallow, cannot see the mist
of breath dancing in front of my face,
so I pirouette, do a shuffle ball
change out of here while I can.

Act One

She crawled out of bed,
showered, carefully selected
her red dress, her red
cut glass earrings,
meticulously applied
her make-up, then stood
before the mirror, surveying
the almost finished product.

Then began her final and
most crucial selection—the mask.
Would she choose the camouflage
of bravery to conceal her fears,
or joy to cover her sorrows,
or perhaps confidence to
obscure her insecurities?

She reached out, pressed
it to her face, hoping the
pretense would last until
once again she was
safely home.

Through the Glass Darkly

The fog tumbles in, dense
and unrelenting,

shrouding my senses
so that I see through

the glass darkly, and I hear
only muffled sounds,

the swish of the tree outside
my window waiting

for the winnowing to come,
and I search for words

but cannot find them,
for they are adrift

inside the cloud
of obscurity.

The last day of her life

She wondered what it would be like,
the last day of her life, wondered
if she would know it was coming,
her last breath, and if she would be
afraid.

She never expected it to be like
this, watching a fly buzzing
around her head, unable to
swat at it, which might not
be a good idea anyway—
what if it were an angel,
waiting to take her
home?

She heard the droning of the
insect, felt the air displaced
around her as it flew ever
closer, and when it landed
on her forehead it felt light
and heavy all at the same
time.

She drew in one ragged
breath, holding it forever
it seemed, and then let
it go, once and for all, she
let everything go, and
looking back, her body
seemed so small in that
bed with white linens,
and the tubing that had
connected her to life
finally, mercifully,

released
and she was flying,
flying high and fast,
just like in her dreams
and she was an old woman
no more, no longer sick,
no longer in pain, but free,
at long last
free.

There is no Organization in Chaos

The universe demands order.
So why is it that so many
people seek chaos, or
if they do not actively
seek it, they certainly
do not avoid it.

The person who coined
the phrase, "organized chaos"
was either five cats short of crazy
or a sadist intent upon
inflicting his own brand
of bedlam upon humankind.

I find that the older I get,
the more order I need.
In fact, do not surprise me,
not with a birthday party
or flowers or even chocolate.
Let me be a part of the

planning process, let me
have some hand in my own
life, whatever life is left,
and then I will be happy,
or at least not unhappy,
for my house will be in order.

This Old House

The house was at the edge of town
and prosperity had left it alone
and neglected, the shutters hanging
precariously, the paint peeling
and the front steps splintered and broken,
betraying the beauty within.

She lived on the edge of sanity
and reason left her alone
and solitary, intimacy not able
to withstand the treason of
broken vows, a crushed heart
refusing to divulge the secrets within.

He worked on the head of a pin,
and dancing with demons left him alone
and embittered, the frequent and tortured
target of miscreants with no other purpose
than stealing his livelihood, killing his joy,
destroying his legacy and the pride within.

Together, the house, the woman, and
the man found themselves in a new
place, a new race to the finish, and
together they found the grace to rebuild
houses and lives in a manner that
restored beauty, love and tranquility.

And all of the people said, "Amen."[9]

Somewhere in Between

There is a place where memories go to sleep,
a place that I imagine is hazy, with the blue
of the sky punching holes in the mist,

insisting that the sun concentrate its light
upon us, showing us the truth, but
the clouds obscure what we know,

what we remember, and it is only
at night, in our dreams, that we
can access the place where memories

dwell and once again become real,
the place that is not among the living,
nor the dead, but somewhere in between.

Salvaging Time

Ten minutes slip into twenty,
twenty wends its way into thirty
and time melts from Dali's canvas
and settles into the cracks between
the pine planks on the bedroom floor.

We wait, because there is nothing
else for us to do.
We try (unsuccessfully) to scoop
up some of the minutes, but they are
rendered useless, polluted by the lint,
dirt and dog hair gathered there.

Warmth rides down on sun's rays
and glides in through the blinds,
finding one corner first,
then reaching out farther
until we lay helpless and exposed
in the light of mid-morning's truth,

still seeking more minutes
since the ticking and tocking
has slowed to an unrecognizable
sound and the second hand jerks
in spasms, soon to move no more.

Playing 'Possum

The road before us is not straight—
I can tell by the way the dotted
yellow lines waggle in front of
me, and the manner in which
the lights of the Cadillac forty
yards ahead zigzag in and out,
back and forth, like a running
back trying for his first touchdown.

The armadillo lounging by the
side of the road sways to the
music of the eighteen wheel
trucks and occasional cars,
wonders what he is doing here,
so close to these messengers
of death, so he tucks his head down
and pretends he is somewhere

else and the trucks and cars
are not there. He bides his
time, knowing that whatever
is on the other side of the road
can wait, and he will live
to cross the highway another day—
perhaps in a place where the road
is straight and only armadillos play.

Perspective

I am a victim of my own pragmatism,
forever searching for the core
of what is instead of reaching
for the pinnacle of what
could be.

My husband sees himself
as one entrenched in optimism,
but is it really optimism to forever
see things the way you want them to be,
or is it delusion?

Benjamin Franklin was a self-professed
pessimist, asserting that optimists
are in constant danger of being
disappointed, while he, on occasion,
was pleasantly surprised.

I can live with pleasant surprise, even
if it is only occasional.

No One is Home

Heartache knocks at my door
but I pretend I am not home,
not willing to suffer any more
for my art or any other thing.

Not that I believe I am the only
one who has ever felt pain,
or that my adversity has
been greater than yours.

I simply choose not to allow
anguish to linger in my
presence any longer—if I
can choose the type of

coffee I drink, why can
I not choose to leave the
door unanswered, to pick
up the Welcome Mat upon

which Heartache wipes his
feet and stow it in the basement,
behind the rakes and shovels
and other things for which I have no use.

I See the Moon and the Moon Sees Me

This is what I know about the moon.

The moon is not comprised of green cheese,
and there is no man taking up residence
in any of its canals or craters.

When I am in Arkansas and the moon
is full and bright, that same moon
shines and illuminates the place
you are in Africa, so although
we are separated by miles
and time zones, we still
see the same full moon
shining down upon us,
on each one of us,
wrapping us in
the comfort of
its sameness.

God bless the moon and God bless you and me.

Down but not out

I feel the heat of summer strapped
onto my back like a straitjacket,
serving to restrict my movements
and turn my breathing shallow.

       I think of you and me and
how we are bound not by anything
so sordid as a jacket with metal
clasps in the back, but something

as simple as an invisible cord, loosely
draped over both our wrists, serving
to remind us that we are forever
joined, forever linked

       in this world and the next.
I only wish we could escape
what can simply be described as
"Arkansas hot," for I can not

bear the boiling temperatures any
longer, not even if our passion
bubbles to the surface as it used to
so often on these steamy Arkansas nights.

Transparency

Blue veins ripple under tissue paper
skin the color of a faded daffodil.
Eyes still alert, a shame, since
no one knows what lingers in her brain.

She once had desires like you and I,
dreams of dancing and holding
an audience in her sway, but those
hopes were dispersed in the light of day.

She told me once she had an affair,
not for love, nor money, but out of
despair. Desperate people
truly do desperate things.

I watch her chest rise and fall,
and the cobweb pattern in the corner
seizes my attention as it sways
with the wind delivered by the ceiling fan.

She looks so small, in the center
of the bed, and I want her suffering
to end, her struggle to be over,
but the blue veins still pump life

and living is distorted to look like this.

The Future carved in stone?

The fortune teller held her hand
for only a minute,
then looked up with a start
and said she had to close
early, she could not sort
out her future today.

The woman left feeling a gnawing
in her heart, a growing
wad of worry in her stomach
that made her wish she hadn't
stopped at the shabby building
on Highway 19, wished she had

not been drawn in by the
six foot sign showing
a black palm, wished
she had just kept driving,
for then she would be
oblivious to tomorrow.

If only the psychic had
taken the time to say
her quick departure
had nothing to do
with the hand she held,
but the stomach virus

causing her insides to quake.

Is that all there is?

I could not help but notice them,
the older couple just two
tables over at IHOP, he
stirring his coffee sweet
and she with a book
held hostage in her hands,
the pages never turning,
a prop serving only to
stifle conversation.
They looked everywhere
except at each other, rage
radiating from her,
indifference billowing
from him.

Watching them was
like driving by a car
wreck—you don't want
to look, but you can't
not look.

Silence is either golden
or it is a black hole
sucking you in—

there is no in between.

Justice

She wonders to herself if it is too late,
too late to be the person she wanted
to be, too late to accomplish her life's
goals.

She wraps herself in truth, her truth,
thinking, believing, the truth will
set you free. But she does not feel
free, never has, maybe never will.

She grapples with reality, the kind
that keeps her awake at night
waiting for it to slip into her bed
and then push her out, onto the floor.

She wonders to herself if it is too soon,
too soon in her life to expect to be treated
fairly, or is it time to surrender her hopes,
her dreams, to bury them in the graveyard of

disappointments, broken hearts, smashed
lives, with monuments telling the world
that life seldom works out the way
we expect, or hope, or dream.

Love means you should learn to say you're sorry

Now you say you're sorry,
but after all of these years of
waiting, anticipating

how it would feel to
actually hear those
words, the tips of my

fingers are numb, I
can hear my heart beating,
quickly, and I have come

to the conclusion that
I must be having a stroke,
for I could not have

heard you right, since the
words, "I'm sorry,"
are not part of your

lexis, never have
been, so I ask you to say
it again, and you repeat,

"I'm sorry I stepped on your toe."

Oh, I thought so.

Until

I sought for happiness long and
hard, thinking that finding it
would bring untold contentment

   until

I realized happiness cannot be
found, like a street or address,
happiness is a state of mind
and, coincidentally, so is
contentment.

I longed for riches thinking
that by achieving them, receiving
them, I would have my heart's desire

   until

I realized riches are merely
the tool through which our
desires can be achieved, and
it is only through hard work
that we receive either riches
or our heart's desire.

I longed for closeness with my
spouse, my best friend, thinking
that would make me a better

person, more complete,

until

I realized I must search for
completion within myself,
and then, only then, can
I become close enough
to another person to
feel, at last, complete.

I should have told you

then, before the twilight enshrouded
the sun in the night,
how the sound of your name,
sends my pulse into flight,
and yes,

I should have told you
then, whispered in the ear that hears
before the morning dew
awakened your fears
how your absence defiles
the space

we call home, how loneliness
and sorrow sing the
nighttime song, and each day I
am sorry, each day
I regret

I should have told you
then, while we lay on the bed
when our moments were fleeting,
I should have told you,
instead

we played the parts of the king
and the fool, you commanding obedience
to prove my devotion, me, plunging ever deeper
into the ocean not of love, but resentment,
I lingered each day

for the love I showed you was repeatedly
turned away. But I did not know until
love came back in vain, when I touched you

the substance was nothing
more than rain
on a windshield that is
soon wiped away, for the baggage
we carried was scuffed, torn and ruined,
and instead of abandoning it
we carried it on

like it mattered more than
anything else we could amass,
why didn't we throw it into
the great morass of things
now past,

why let it live on, to control and contort,
to muddy our feelings, to continue to distort
the fragile cord of closeness we both should have known,
why couldn't either of us soften
our heart of stone?

        I should tell you
now, or is it too late,
you were always enough,
your presence filled my plate
with comfort

though you never could see,
it was you who needed more,
you needed more than just me, so tonight
I look skyward and with
one final breath,

        I tell you I love
you, I tell you the truth,
the love of my sunset
is still the love from my
youth.[10]

One Woman's Sojourn

Stumbling through the darkness
of confusion,
tumbling into the light of reason
she questioned everything
she had been raised to believe.

She loved God, always had
but science taught
her to look elsewhere for answers
and no one told her some puzzles
have no ready solutions.

So she slipped silently
from her raft
of faith and into the blue-black
waters of the intellect, where
logic alone bobs to the surface.

She turned her back on the God
of her father,
and set out on a journey of
self-actualization, a pilgrimage
she continues to this day.

She still uses phrases like,
"Thank God," although
more out of habit than belief.
She teaches her child we are each
some cosmic accident

and that is sad, I think,
but I believe
that children have the knowledge
of God even before they have reason
to believe, or the ability to reason.

I pray that she will find
her way, that God
will intervene some day
and she will return to that
first love a child has for her Father.

For the first love is
the best love,
and we should not be detoured
on the pathway to righteousness,
not by science, nor reason, nor any other thing.[11]

Soliloquy

I form the street with every step I take,
walking carefully, heel to toe, heel to toe,
the darkness presses in on me,
but it cannot overtake me
as long as I do not go

too far into the shadows, the mist a
lake of swirling eddies, clinging now, singing now
bringing peace upon me,
waiting to console me,
I'm finished now, I take a bow

for the performance is almost over,
words run out, nothing left to do or say,
the spotlight rests upon me
and now all you can see is me,
turning my back and walking away.

Reminiscence

Light filters in through cut glass
windows and prisms of color
fall quietly on the floor.

Dust particles ride on rays of sun
sneaking in through slatted blinds
and I am a child again, batting

at the dust, causing it to swirl
and dance around the room,
and I dance, too, laughing

and twirling with arms reaching
wide, and I am spinning
like a top until, overcome with

dizziness, I topple right over
and all that is left is light
and dust and me.

The Trials of Job

I have known women who pitter-patter
around problems in soft-soled shoes,
thinking that by ignoring their hardships
they will simply disappear.

I am not one of those women.

I rail against life's injustices, thinking,
believing
that surely God will hear my cries
and deliver me from yet another insult borne
of fate, or ill timing, or perhaps just
the whim of my fellow man.

It does not happen.

Job knew how to take his medicine without
a lump of sugar, but I insist at least on
a glass of wine at the end of the day,
to maybe lessen the whine at the tail end
of the trial and then maybe, just maybe,
I can face tomorrow hoping for a better
outcome to a certain causality.

The Journey Takes You Home

Think hope is gone, you
can't go on, the destination
too far, the road too hard?
    Remember,
your journey will take you home.

Think life is unfair,
the scales broken beyond repair,
too late, nothing to remunerate?
    Remember,
your journey will take you home.

Think bad times are all you know,
life's twists and turns left you
broken, too many dreams unspoken?
    Remember,
your journey will take you home.

At the end of the day, you
will look back and say,
it is done, I was able to carry on.
    I remembered,
my journey was only to take me home.

Endnotes

[i]   "White Towels," Richard Jones, Poetry 180, A Turning Back to Poetry, p. 42, Billy Collins, Ed., 2003.

[ii]   W. H. Auden. (n.d.). BrainyQuote.com. Retrieved July 15, 2010, from BrainyQuote.com Web site: HYPERLINK "http://www.brainyquote.com/quotes/quotes/w/whauden146093.html" http://www.brainyquote.com/quotes/quotes/w/whauden146093.html

[iii] "The Quotations Page."Jane Austen, "Mansfield Park." Ed. Michael Moncur. HYPERLINK "http://www.quotationspage.com" www.quotationspage.com 4/18/2008.

[iv]   "Wikiquote." Henry David Thoreau, "Journals-1838-1859)Wikimedia Foundation, Inc. HYPERLINK "http://en.wikiquote.org/wiki/Henry_David_Thoreau Journals_.281838-1859.29" http://en.wikiquote.org/wiki/Henry_David_Thoreau Journals_.281838-1859.29 4/18/2008.

[v]   My Creative Writing instructor, Professor Ralph Burns, warned against sentimentality in a poem as "something only God would care about." I think he did not take into account mothers. While this is clearly a sentimental poem, I can live with that.

[vi]   This poem is in response to Obama's request to Prime Minister Netanyahu to refrain from using the phrase, "next year in Jerusalem," the traditional closing to the Jewish Seder because it is too contentious.

[vii] Esther 4:14 paraphrased

[viii] Neda Agha-Soltan was murdered by a sniper on June 20, 2009 in Iran as she joined with others to protest what they believed to be a fraudulent election.

[ix]   A poem born from a writing exercise.The exercise was to write a 7 line stanza about an old house, but after completing the assignment, I realized the poem was not finished. So, I let the poem go where it needed to go.

[x]   In honor of the actors and the director of The Weekend Theater's production of "Rent"

[xi]   Written after watching the monologue "Letting Go of God" by Julie Sweeney.

Carol J. Grace resides in Arkansas with her husband, Larry, and their four legged family Zoe, Chloe, Hercules and Cassie. They are active in their church, Asbury United Methodist Church, and Carol is available for speaking engagements. You may contact her at reflections.poetry@comcast.net.

LaVergne, TN USA
04 January 2011
210907LV00005B/2/P